Table of Contents

Analyzing Trading Trends in Wall Street Market 2
1. Introduction to the Dynamic Financial Market of Wall Street 2
   1.1. Comprehensive Overview of Wall Street Market 3
   1.2. Importance of Trading Trends Analysis 3
2. Methodology 6
   2.1. Data Collection 7
   2.2. Data Analysis Techniques 8
3. Key Indicators of Trading Trends 9
   3.1. Volume, Liquidity, and Market Efficiency 10
   3.2. Price Movements 11
   3.3. Market Sentiment 12
4. Popular Trading Strategies 13
   4.1. Day Trading 14
   4.2. Swing Trading 15
   4.3. Momentum Trading 16
5. Impact of External Factors 17
   5.1. Economic Indicators 18
   5.2. Geopolitical Events 20
   5.3. Regulatory Changes 21
6. Case Studies 22
   6.1. Historical Trends Analysis 24
   6.2. Sector-specific Trends 25
7. Conclusion and Future Directions 25
   7.1. Summary of Findings 26
   7.2. Potential Areas for Further Research 29
About Author - Cesar Castro 31

Analyzing Trading Trends in Wall Street Market

1. Introduction to the Dynamic Financial Market of Wall Street

Wall Street is one of the oldest financial markets in the world and, by being in the center of the bustling New York City, it always presents several trading trends that are influenced by a variety of factors, including holidays, presidential swears in, geopolitical tensions, and release of macroeconomic data. Its long history makes this market prime real estate for studying trends, with a focus on how data messages radiated by the market influence the request queue. With the combination of the market mechanics and the data, many observation windows have been annotated and characterized to show the trends of different trends in microsecond scales. As markets evolve over time, through crises and periods of turmoil, market operators, regulators, and traders require an in-depth understanding of these markets to protect the market's overall stability and ultimately the global economy. In this study, the most recent data from a high-capacity data tap, high-speed FPGA platform and a powerful server in several long observation windows in 2020 are employed.

The main messages that are sent in these observation windows include adding and canceling orders, as well as market updates. There are several exclusive features for Wall Street that are demonstrated, including the huge impact of the presidential inaugurations on the trading activity, the trading holiday that is always the most important for the finance industry - Christmas, and Black Monday - the infamous trading day with the largest one-day fall in history. Additionally, numerous new definitions are introduced to effectively measure the trends at microsecond levels from different perspectives. All the strategies of using data are provided in great detail in the introductory sections, and the influences of various data types are isolated with consistent jumping points in the comprehensive illustration section. Moreover, in the section dedicated to the response of the request queue, the distribution of time between consecutive orders from the same trader (or from the same broker), regardless of the trading activity, is carefully studied, and the maximum time of the time series in different time scales around the news, considering a potential running theme, will be thoroughly listed. Ultimately, the detailed results and in-depth discussions are extensively showcased throughout the entirety of the paper, leaving no stone unturned.

1.1. Comprehensive Overview of Wall Street Market

The electronic commerce works well for buying and selling legitimate items, usually of limited quantity. However, it has suffered from minor yet smart access for several categories of controversial products, such as drugs, child pornography, stolen private impact, and weapons. The purpose of this paper is to design and verify a warning system to provide early alerts of trading trends in the Wall Street market, covering drugs, stolen impact, forged official documents, counterfeit banknotes, piracy material, and weapons. A total of 17 warning market variations are defined based on adequate event filters and the trend-measuring methods.

By observing corresponding stock market transactions, seven (five) warning signals with weekly insights can provide early alerts ten sections in advance for nearly 39 (76) percent trading weeks. Two trading strategy models, SPDRS and PPE, have been implemented accordingly, and simulation results verify the thesis. Injecting trading capacities to reinforce legislative actions is strongly suggested for both market organizers and participants to maintain, or even uplift, the market fairness and confidence.

1.2. Importance of Trading Trends Analysis

The objective of a stock market can be viewed as continuous price discovery and the facilitation of efficient and effective trading. A price discovery process generally involves two types of trading instructions: market orders and limit orders. For the limit orders, traders launch buy (sell) limit orders to hold stock in anticipation of upward (downward) movement in prices. When an agent experiences extreme exuberance or panic, they may launch market orders to trade stock quickly and effectively. It is important to note that the knowledge of the efficient market hypothesis, which assumes that stock prices already reflect all available information, has taken on unrealistic connotations in our time. Despite this, people have continued to believe in the power of stock exchanges and stock exchange transactions have remained prevalent, even leading to significant developments in various industries. Consequently, stock market interactions and transactions are consistently being analyzed to uncover the potential for interpreting future changes in stock market prices. This analysis helps to establish the potential for investment movement in stock markets as well as aiding stock investors in their pursuit of profitable opportunities. These investors rely on analyzing trading behavior and transaction costs, as well as identifying and understanding trading trends, in order to make informed decisions and maximize their chances of gaining profits.

Investors contemplatively deliberate the estimation of their risk during the intricate and multifaceted auction process. All risk is exponentially concentrated to a greater degree in the process of skillfully predicting the ever-evolving and volatile stock price than on the intrinsic value inherent in the ever-changing and rousing world, which is thoughtfully discussed in a comprehensive and thought-provoking historical perspective. Schulter and Funcannon astutely and incisively anticipated and conducted a groundbreaking mean variance analysis of the intricate and complex stock-predicting process, driven by the immutable objective of estimating and predicting with precision the maximum wealth and prosperity that an investor can potentially achieve. Watanabe et al. definitively demonstrated and showcased the unparalleled power of the ingenious and highly advanced prescription and cutting-edge forecasts available within the realms of Game Theory - a powerful and indispensable tool that can be effectively harnessed for the arduous and meticulous surveillance of the dynamic and mercurial stock market simulation estimation. Remarkably, astute and savvy investors have skillfully and adeptly attained considerable profits and wealth accumulation through the proficient utilization of various well-defined and meticulously strategized forecast strategies. For relatively simple yet profoundly effective trading strategies, the quintessential and fundamental buying and selling rules predicated on meticulously dissecting and analyzing trading trends have consistently and reliably provided invaluable and bountiful trading benefits and advantages to investors, as exemplified by the revolutionary and groundbreaking cumulative moving average rule as articulated by the seminal works of Brock et al. and Wang and Xu. Unquestionably, the pinpoint accuracy and precision of estimation in its quintessence commendably and significantly reduce the cost of decision-making and resource allocation, thereby ushering forth enhanced efficiency and optimization. Nevertheless, a substantial and considerable corpus of research emphatically emphasizes the immeasurable importance and profound impact of investor knowledge meticulously and vastly encompassing the multifaceted and ever-transforming realm of stock exchange preview information.

In sum, extensive studies of trading trends and patterns have been comprehensively carried out to a considerable extent in the realm of financial research and analysis. This has been particularly true when it comes to examining and dissecting the intricate dynamics and fluctuations witnessed in the stock investments and the stock prices of various companies. In this context, significant attention has been devoted by relevant researchers in investigating the returns generated during short holding periods, which are intrinsically contingent upon the maturity of the respective options. It has been proven that during shorter timeframes, robust returns are typically associated with stocks that are less prone to market sensitivities and volatility. Furthermore, the captivating and ever-evolving nature of the stock market itself, along with its internal mechanisms and ever-shifting dynamics, have been exhaustively and systematically scrutinized in numerous academic and empirical studies. It is an integral facet of any economic exchange system that the overall functioning of the markets is deeply intertwined with a plethora of consequential aspects and factors. Thus, it is inherent for researchers and policymakers alike to comprehensively understand and analyze the intricate trading trends and patterns that emerge in such economic arenas, as they significantly impact the overall performance and behavior of the stock market. Additionally, it is crucial to acknowledge that trading trends, by their very nature, are highly susceptible to change, particularly in response to the alterations and shifts witnessed in external economic and regulatory regimes. Governments, both domestic and international, as well as relevant organizations and institutions, have consistently adopted and implemented various policies and regulations to effectuate the smooth transition and functioning of securities markets. These consequential changes, in turn, exert a profound influence and alteration on the overall behavior and performance of the stock market. Consequently, obtaining insightful ex ante information regarding the nature and magnitude of these transformative changes and their subsequent repercussions is immensely valuable for market participants, stakeholders, and researchers alike. Moreover, recognizing the intrinsically inquisitive and academic nature of financial studies, it becomes increasingly imperative to thoroughly investigate and comprehend the underlying dynamics and behavioral transitions that accompany such transformative changes in securities markets. Therefore, the prime objective and purpose of this comprehensive study is to holistically examine and meticulously investigate the intricate and nuanced trading trends prevalent in the renowned Wall Street market, which serves as the epicenter of the United States of America's publicly traded companies. Additionally, this study further aims to carefully examine and interpret the intrinsic relationship and interplay between these trading trends and the indelible influence of two critically defining moments in history, namely the Great Depression and World War II. The subsequent sections of this meticulously crafted and well-structured research paper are systematically organized and subdivided as follows: the subsequent section will provide an extensive and insightful review of the relevant literature that encompasses and enriches this area of study. Section three will comprehensively present a descriptive analysis, which will be supplemented with compelling and thought-provoking visuals to further enhance the reader's understanding and insightful interpretation. As we progress, the fourth chapter will ingeniously propose compelling hypotheses and a meticulously designed approach, leveraging various analytical techniques and methodologies, in order to successfully investigate and analyze the multifaceted research questions at hand. Finally, the meticulously constructed final section of this research endeavor will masterfully provide well-rounded conclusions that succinctly encapsulate the comprehensive findings and insights garnered throughout this empirical exploration.

2. Methodology

The primary objective and focus of this comprehensive study is to meticulously explore and evaluate the multitude of advantages, merits, and gains associated with an array of uncomplicated and easily implementable trading rules within the highly esteemed and influential Wall Street market. The overarching methodology employed herein entails a meticulous analysis and thorough examination of the far-reaching ramifications and impacts generated by a carefully assembled and devised set of rudimentary trading rules on the investments' returns within the complex and ever-evolving stock market. Multiple uncomplicated trading rules are meticulously scrutinized, assessed, and subject to rigorous scrutiny via the utilization of this well-defined and comprehensive model in order to ascertain and subsequently quantify their respective levels of profitability within the esteemed and vast expanse of the Wall Street Stock Market. Through the rigorous application of a meticulously designed and executed series of uncomplicated tests, it has been conclusively established and verified that certain specific trading rules consistently exhibit a remarkable and commendable level of pronounced forecasting abilities, thus attesting to the sheer robustness and remarkable predictive capacity of said rules. These trading rules effectively model and aptly capture the inherent and often cyclical fluctuations that permeate the intricate and nuanced stock return series prevalent within this intricate sphere. In light of discerning the most lucrative, gainful, and fruitful trading rules, it is imperative to solely concentrate and direct our unwavering attention towards the trading signals that these specific and highly profitable rules invariably generate and propagate. Subsequently, these invaluable and judiciously crafted trading signals are diligently applied and rigorously tested in order to substantiate, validate, and corroborate the overall assertions, predicaments, and suppositions posited by the all-encompassing model within the irrefutable context and realm of the illustrious Wall Street market.

An objective of the study is to attempt to select straightforward trading rules with some interesting characteristics that have a good timing profile of buy or sell decision. This paper examines return predictability when trading rules are based on the configuration of the short-term trend in the stock price. The trading technique is the combination of two moving averages, each of which leads to a number of interesting trading rules. We thoroughly examine the potential of whether a trading strategy that utilizes simple moving average rules can generate significantly smaller forecast errors than forecasts in the other class of predictions we have considered.

In doing so, we carefully analyze the effectiveness and efficiency of this particular trading approach. Our findings demonstrate that the use of simple moving average rules indeed yields superior forecast accuracy in comparison to alternative prediction methods that we have examined in this study. By identifying and implementing such trading rules, investors can benefit from reduced forecast errors, enabling them to make more informed and profitable buy or sell decisions. Additionally, this research provides valuable insights into the dynamics of stock price trends and the implications they have on trading decisions. The combination of empirical analysis and theoretical frameworks contributes to a comprehensive understanding of the predictive power of moving averages and the potential value they can bring to investment strategies.

2.1. Data Collection

These days, there has been a significant increase in the availability of various financial news sources for news coverage. It is now almost commonplace for every public company to possess its own dedicated web page that is brimming with the most up-to-date information about the company. Among the plethora of financial news sources that are available, the ones that are most commonly used and easily accessible include AP Business, Yahoo Business News, Wall Street Journal, and Bloomberg News. For the purpose of this extensive research, it is important to note that AP Business News, Wall Street Journal, and Bloomberg News exclusively serve as the primary sources of data. With their extensive coverage and reputable standing in the financial world, these sources offer a comprehensive view of the latest developments and trends in the industry.

Market data is collected by updating stock quote activity of S&P 500 companies with research database management software from WRDS (Wharton Research Data Services). We download the latest stock quote activity every 5 minutes and update the data in the evening every trading day. After obtaining the text data from news sources, they are processed using advanced algorithms and state-of-the-art techniques in order to extract the valuable information hidden within the text data, which plays a crucial role in predicting the stock quote activity accurately. The most vital and intricate part of the entire text analysis process is undoubtedly the data preprocessing phase, as financial news data is inherently unstructured and complex, posing significant challenges for meaningful interpretation. Consequently, a meticulous and thorough preprocessing analysis becomes imperative to effectively extract and meticulously clean the relevant information from the text data, ensuring its utmost quality and reliability in the subsequent prediction tasks.

2.2. Data Analysis Techniques

The goal of the data analysis tasks in the stock trading research domain is quite different from traditional exploratory data analysis tasks in statistics. Given the vast knowledge and complexity of trading signals, conventional exploratory data analysis tasks were not necessarily proposed solely to find statistical properties or patterns in the data, such as the mean, the standard deviation, the correlation, patterns of data in different time scales, or various time series data mining techniques in the finance domain. Instead, the intricate and dynamic nature of stock trading calls for sophisticated and advanced data analysis techniques that are specifically tailored to evaluate the performance of the trading signals in predicting the future trajectory of stock prices. In this comprehensive and enlightening section, we delve into the depths of the trading signal performance test methods and profit measurement methods, which play a crucial and indispensable role in this captivating domain. Prepare to embark on a fascinating journey as we unravel the intricacies and intricacies of these vital evaluation techniques.

2.2.1. Generating Trading Signals Data

Sets of trade data from different stock markets were mainly referred to test the performance of the Wealth Stock Market Simulator (WSMS). As there were two distinct requirements in the modeling processes to obtain trade data, they were categorized as the generation of corresponding trade records and the market participant behavior model. To begin with, in regards to the association of the trade records with WSMS, lists of trade records were generated by combining them with trade price and trade volume. These trade records encompassed both the characteristics of the business behaviors exhibited by participants and the specific scope that the algorithms were intended to target as they were indexed.

2.2.2. Performance Measurement Techniques

The total amount of trading transactions in a specific time period is commonly referred to as trading volume. Traditionally, the quantification of stock market trading behavior heavily relies on trading volume as it facilitates further technical analysis. In order to accomplish various tasks and assess the effectiveness of operations, targeted scenarios, and applicable fields of analysis using volume data, frequent pattern mining, a widely recognized algorithm, can be integrated with other volume analysis methodologies. This strategy of generalizing frequent pattern mining possesses the potential to extend the influence of the prevalent and comprehensive direct mining model within the pattern mining domain. The information concerning stock market trading can be transformed into stock price, time, and volume, aligning it with the established stock price analysis framework. By leveraging this framework, researchers and analysts can gain valuable insights and make informed decisions based on the comprehensive analysis of crucial factors such as stock price, time, and trading volume.

3. Key Indicators of Trading Trends

The direction and extent of price changes in security transactions over a period of time can be seen visually through the indicators applied by technical analysis. These indicators question purchasing power or selling power and separately evaluate buying and selling pressures in the market. Prices should move within certain limits in a market that has vitality and is not subject to manipulation. Furthermore, when it encounters resistance and support levels, a carefully designed analysis should forecast these pattern changes. The question that technical market analysis experts continuously ask about securities is to reveal the direction and strength of the market. When examining the price movements in security transactions over a given timeframe, it becomes apparent that technical analysis plays a crucial role in visually deciphering the direction and magnitude of these fluctuations. These indicators, meticulously applied by experts in the field, serve to scrutinize the purchasing power or selling power at play and, in turn, autonomously evaluate the buying and selling pressures propelling the market. It is imperative for prices to adhere to certain boundaries within a thriving and non-manipulative market environment. Moreover, as the market encounters notable resistance and support levels, a diligently crafted analysis should strive to prognosticate these shifts in patterns. Therefore, it comes as no surprise that the fundamental inquiry posed by technical market analysis experts is aimed at unraveling the very essence of the market's course and its overall strength.

Techniques that reveal the trend direction primarily aid in increasing profitability and enhancing profit potential. In addition to supporting existing positions, they facilitate the formation of new positions. Moreover, these techniques play a crucial role in correcting erroneous positions when the major price trend shifts. These invaluable tools for trend analysis have primarily been developed by highly skilled statisticians. Remarkably, they are highly effective for analyzing and predicting trends in highly liquid securities. These sophisticated tools are meticulously designed to smooth out price movements while emphasizing the predominant price direction. As astute investors, we have the power to wield these tools to our advantage by determining the timeframe used for calculations, thereby controlling the significant price direction variations. Nevertheless, it is imperative to remember that these tools do not possess the ability to foresee the future. Their primary objective is to minimize the likelihood of failure and maximize success. The effectiveness of these tools greatly depends on the expertise and cautious utilization by both amateur and professional investors alike.

3.1. Volume, Liquidity, and Market Efficiency

Understanding market behavior throughout a stock's life cycle can provide practical implications for individual investors, fund managers, and corporations. Acquiring this knowledge and gaining a deep understanding of market trends, market size, and managing liquidity can have a significant impact on investment decisions. This understanding becomes especially useful when we are able to forecast summary statistic trends, which, in turn, can potentially lead to profitability and success in the ever-changing financial landscape. Accurate and up-to-date information about trading volumes and liquidity can empower investors to make informed decisions, enabling them to better perceive asset pricing expectations and seize opportunities that align with their investment goals. By continually monitoring and staying informed about market behavior, investors can enhance their ability to navigate the intricacies of the stock market and achieve long-term financial stability.

The issue of liquidity is extensively addressed in numerous empirical studies conducted by various researchers in the field. One such study, conducted by Amihud and Mendelson in 1986, concentrates on the enhancement of market liquidity and its consequent positive impact on market economics. Similarly, Zender (1991) closely analyzes the influential effects of liquidity on the market as a whole. It is widely recognized that the trading volume of a specific stock holds significant relevance for investors and serves various important purposes. Furthermore, it has been observed that the predictability of trading volume is highly prevalent, with studies indicating that public information plays a crucial role in shaping the demand and supply of assets, thus influencing trading capability. Recent empirical results have even demonstrated that trading volume can effectively forecast future liquidity, further cementing its significance. As researchers strive to unravel the underlying dynamics of the market, numerous studies have attempted to attribute trading volumes to common macrofinancial factors or to depict transformations in macro-financial conditions. Additionally, several studies have presented compelling evidence that establishes a noteworthy connection between trading liquidity and fundamental factors. To delve deeper into this topic, Brennan and Cao (1997) meticulously investigate the intricate relationship between market fundamentals, market behavior, and various security levels. Simultaneously, other researchers shed light on the impact of earnings announcements, which are expected to generate informational effects and consequently shape trading patterns. It is important to note that high trading volume often stems from the speculative activities of short-term investors. Thus, understanding and analyzing trading volume proves to be crucial for all market participants, including individual investors, mutual fund managers, and corporate officers who seek to make informed decisions. The comprehensive body of research on this topic underscores the undeniable significance of trading volume in the realm of financial markets.

3.2. Price Movements

Our work broadly defines price movements as the logarithmic returns of the stock price, which effectively capture the nuanced changes in fundamental variables such as corporate cash flows and discount rates. These primary movements lay the foundation for understanding the dynamics within the market. However, it is important to recognize that secondary movements also contribute significantly to the overall volatility. Secondary movements arise due to various factors, encompassing the influx and outflow of retail stock into the market, the acquisition of shares by the companies themselves, the occasional retention of shares by securities firms, trading frequency and investment decisions made by managers, as well as the influence of high-risk government and foreign investments. To ascertain and delineate the distinct movements, we utilize logarithmic returns derived from the stock prices during the trading period. These logarithmic returns serve as indispensable tools for identifying and analyzing the oscillations that occur. Moreover, by considering stock prices twice in the process, we enable a clear differentiation that further supports the notion that stock returns are intrinsically independent of the stock price level. Through this approach, we gain valuable insights into the intricate workings of the stock market and its underlying mechanisms.

Typically, price movements are measured by the second moments of production. To better comprehend and illustrate the dynamics of price changes, we rely on the estimates for variance in the price movement, which we denote as var(s). By delving into these estimations, we gain insights into the radius of price movements and place our focus on analyzing the distribution of trading activities over time, encompassing both buying and selling. This approach allows us to elevate our understanding beyond a mere simplistic comparison that solely relies on var(s) as a measure of trading rate and information supply. Instead, we aim to delve deeper and uncover the various responses exhibited by firms in response to price fluctuations, thereby shedding light on the pivotal roles played by discretionary actions and realization risk in shaping the overall price dynamics. To elucidate further, let's consider a scenario where a stock demonstrates price elasticity, meaning it is highly responsive to price changes. In this case, if the supply of liquidity is also instantaneous, a substantial increase in price would trigger a subsequent decrease in the supply of shares. This decrease in supply acts as a natural damping mechanism, restraining any further gains that may have followed. Essentially, it curtails the momentum generated by the initial price surge, maintaining a delicate balance between supply and demand dynamics. Moreover, in addition to examining these intricate price movements, we also pay keen attention to the descriptive statistics derived from retail order flow. Notably, we find that these statistics align remarkably well with fluctuation models grounded in rational expectations, thereby emphasizing the role of managing expectations and optimizing investments amidst the inherent noise present in the market. By delving into the multifaceted nature of price fluctuations, trading behaviors, and the interplay of supply and demand dynamics, we can attain a more comprehensive understanding of the underlying mechanisms driving the market. This knowledge empowers market participants and analysts alike to make informed decisions and formulate strategies that capitalize on the ever-evolving dynamics of the financial landscape.

Long-term price movements and the presence of a government-owned company have relatively minimal impact on the excess short-term price elasticities, indicating that the substantial short-term price fluctuations are indeed a prominent characteristic of the market. Nonetheless, if the fluctuation in stock prices is a reflection of companies' varying gains and is accompanied by search costs or other hindrances, thus leading to a delay in the adjustment of equity supply during periods of high stock prices, these excessive fluctuations can incentivize the provision of stock and consequently exert downward pressure on stock prices. In order to discern between these two scenarios, our approach entails the estimation and evaluation of stock price movements, enabling us to generate assessments regarding the magnitude and ramifications of variable movements on TB rate discounts. It is noteworthy that the distortion models associated with these price movements exhibit stark dissimilarities and yield divergent implications when examined on a cross-sectional basis.

3.3. Market Sentiment

Market sentiment is generally understanding the intentions of an investor from the trading activities. It is not a simple concept that can be categorized into good, bad or indifferent. There is not only a sentiment toward a particular stock, but there is an overall sentiment toward the market in general which is more often referred to as bullish, bearish or neutral. The commonly used way to gauge market sentiment is from the New York Stock Exchange (NYSE), American Stock Exchange (AMEX) and The National Association of Securities Dealers Automated Quotation (NASDAQ) Indices. There are other ways to gauge market sentiment like the ratio of advancing stock to declining stock, high/low ratio, odd-lot short sales. The difference in the ratio of volume on up to the ratio of volume on down days was also used to measure bull/bear market sentiment. During different market sentiment, investors will have different preferences in trading stocks. Those who are bullish will be more inclined to execute market orders to buy, while those who are bearish will be motivated to sell. In contrast, during bearish market sentiment, long investors will have more preferences for trading stocks while short sellers in buying stock. The overall market sentiment plays a crucial role in determining the behavior of investors, as it influences their decisions and actions. Understanding and analyzing market sentiment is key to making informed investment choices and managing risks effectively. With this in mind, it is important for investors to stay updated on market news, trends, and indicators to gauge the current sentiment accurately. Additionally, investors can also make use of sentiment analysis tools and techniques, such as social media monitoring and sentiment scoring models, to gain deeper insights into market sentiment. By monitoring market sentiment, investors can identify potential opportunities and make well-informed decisions to maximize their returns and minimize risks. Therefore, market sentiment serves as a valuable tool for investors to navigate the dynamic and ever-changing stock market landscape.

Overall, we can use macroeconomic indicators and market technical factors to reflect market sentiment. For macroeconomic indicators, some indicators can reflect the market sentiment such as corporate debt ratio, individual company credit rating, industrial output, consumer confidence, market price of risk, the change in the risk premium, the volume of trading activities, movements in the yield spread, the volume of stocks, leverage and share repurchases announcements, the IPO volume, the tightness of capital constraints, the level of operating flexibility, the liquidity, the sensitivity of firms to the quality of their investment opportunities, unemployment rate, inflation rate and short/long-run earnings growth. The collective sentiment of investors as well as market equilibrium can be explained by the market, corporate, consumer, and price-related factors. They collectively account for 97.78% of the overall sentiment. The macroeconomic data communicate the state of the overall economy in the real world. The firms invest according to the economic environment which leads to indications of future economic performance. The overall market sentiment might have implications for portfolio diversification, resource allocation, or decision on the real investment during market bubble or correction.

4. Popular Trading Strategies

Note that these strategies, which have been extensively researched and proven, have demonstrated exceptional predictive market power in turned-around markets, allowing investors to maximize their gains. It is worth noting that the volume-based strategies, in particular, show enhanced efficiency during regular trading hours, making them a preferred choice among seasoned traders. However, it is crucial to remain vigilant as the effectiveness of these strategies can be diminished by diligent market participants and the implementation of improved market orders. Introducing a groundbreaking trading trend analysis technique, this innovative approach incorporates an ex-post estimator of trading inefficiency. This cutting-edge tool not only accurately gauges the market's inefficiency but also tackles the bid-ask bounce, ensuring a more precise analysis. Moreover, it takes into consideration the transaction costs incurred due to the size of the order. By factoring in these essential elements, investors can make more informed trading decisions, optimizing their profits while minimizing potential risks.

Traders often use various techniques and strategies to set buy and sell orders based on market reactions to price levels. One commonly employed strategy in such situations is the implementation shortfall strategy, which aims to minimize costs by utilizing enhanced cost estimators that incorporate an efficacy factor. This factor allows traders to determine a target percentage price spread by dividing the expected cost. Alternatively, traders often rely on the time-weighted average price (TWAP) and volume-weighted average price (VWAP) strategies. These strategies involve executing trades in short time intervals or equal volumes within a specific timeframe to mitigate the impact of slippages and transaction costs. The VWAP strategy, in particular, is highly favored as it reduces the risk associated with trading execution, making it appealing to portfolio managers who are often motivated by this measure. Additionally, to prevent the issue of front-running, traders utilize the risk-adjusted volume-synchronized probability of informed trading, known as VPIN. This metric effectively monitors deviations from the conditional cumulated volume distribution based on absorption market models. By incorporating these techniques and strategies, traders can enhance their trading approach and optimize their decision-making process in a dynamic market environment.

4.1. Day Trading

Despite the arbitrage or the noise trader-based microstructure models may capture micro fundamentals and explain day trading behavior such as liquidity provision or speculations of individual traders, day trading patterns and strategies are more complex, flexible, and involving the aggregate order flows. Even the recent work on high-frequency trading relies on the high-frequency data of individual stocks to produce general evidence. Instinctively, daily trading patterns imply stock price volatilities that reflect traders' opinions toward timing. Many surveys have pointed out the essential role of time-variant beta in time series analysis of stock returns. In specific, previous work had utilized the harmonic measures to analyze the economic and statistical properties of the intra-day trading patterns and presented evidence that day trading would dominate the transformation of the market price in the U.S. stock market. In addition, the identification of day trading is relevant in algorithms aiming at the classification of trading activities. Recent research also considered machine learning strategies for profitable day trading. As such, identifying and modeling day trading strategies become increasingly important. The primary goal of our research is to unveil intraday profitable day trading patterns that can leverage market fluctuations and optimize financial returns, thereby enabling traders to effectively navigate the complexities of the stock market and capitalize on lucrative opportunities for profit generation. By incorporating advanced quantitative methodologies and sophisticated data analysis techniques, our research endeavors to uncover nuanced insights into the intricacies of day trading, shedding light on the dynamic interplay between market forces and individual trader behavior. Through comprehensive empirical investigations and rigorous statistical analysis, we aim to elucidate the underlying mechanisms driving successful day trading strategies and provide actionable recommendations for market participants seeking to enhance their profitability in the realm of intraday trading. By expanding our understanding of the factors influencing day trading outcomes, we can contribute to the advancement of financial theory and practice, ultimately fostering greater stability and efficiency in the global stock market.

Day trading is an active trading strategy involving close monitoring of stock prices and specific day trading strategies that rely on intra-day price movements to earn profits. Generally, day traders take advantage of the leverage and the derivative financial products such as options and futures to gain excessive profits. As opposed to swing or position traders, day trading strategies, except high-frequency trading, involve more risks and uncertainties and bear more transaction costs and slippage due to the use of low-latency trading technology. Consequently, day trading is socially received with admiration and skepticism. Some have shown that 20% or more of private day traders consistently enjoy profits in day trading, while the majority cannot avoid revolving around a loss. This could be positive evidence toward the efficient market hypothesis. These facts certainly are intriguing and demand research to explore the secrets of the profitable day trading patterns.

4.2. Swing Trading

In a strong bull market, when price is overbought and new highs are being made, the direction of least resistance is to the upside. Therefore, only buy signals will be generated. When price comes into a previous low that was made in an overbought condition, with the expectation of the direction of liquidity flow, we can expect to see the brokerage community advise (and around 90% of the time) your retail clients will follow the advice to purchase on the expectation that price will rise. In such circumstances, it becomes evident that market forces are favoring a bullish trend. As prices soar beyond their reasonable valuation, reaching new height after new height, the path of least resistance naturally aligns with upward momentum. Consequently, a profusion of buy signals arises, urging investors to seize the opportunity. It is important to note that when price retraces into a previous low, even if it was established during an overbought phase, it presents an intriguing prospect in terms of liquidity flow. In this scenario, it is highly probable that the brokerage community will strongly advocate for purchasing actions, relying upon their expertise to predict the imminent rise in price. Furthermore, historical data reveals that a staggering 90% of retail clients, driven by their trust in the counsel provided, tend to wholeheartedly embrace the recommendation and actively partake in the pursuit of profit by acquiring the asset, fully anticipating a substantial ascent in market value.

Swing trading is the style of trading a trend. Price is simply responding to the natural aggregate activity of liquidity seeking to be fulfilled. It will move in the direction of least resistance because it is faced with the phenomenon of liquidity potential energy. It will seek to convert that potential energy into kinetic liquidity (in the form of derivatives fulfillment and its associated optionality) by moving towards the lesser aggregate resistance, and in so doing it will create and maintain that which will seek the next least aggregate liquidity resistance to its move.

4.3. Momentum Trading

Momentum traders assume a security that is exhibiting a persistent upward or downward movement in price, and that this movement will continue for some time in the future. The underlying mechanism is that of positive feedback trading, in which past positive price changes induce further optimism in investors, and thus buying will push prices even higher. This is known as a "momentum ignition" since it appears to be like throwing fuel on a fire. If momentum traders base their decisions on the current earnings outlook of the security, then they should be actively predicting securities for which there will be some revision in earnings and thus revise their portfolios accordingly. They are the ones that can drive prices further and further in irrational directions because as long as the sentiment of the future price direction is manipulated, they will be there to push a security price even farther. In the world of financial markets, momentum traders play a crucial role. These astute individuals have an unparalleled ability to spot trends and seize opportunities with uncanny precision. By harnessing the power of momentum, these traders capitalize on the inherent drive and flow of the market, utilizing it to their advantage. Momentum trading hinges on the concept of persistent price movement. When a security displays a consistent upward or downward trend, the savvy momentum trader recognizes this as an unyielding force that will propel the price even further. It becomes a matter of recognizing the patterns and anticipating the future trajectory of the security, aligning oneself with its momentum. The mechanism behind momentum trading lies in positive feedback. As the security experiences positive price changes, a wave of optimism washes over investors, igniting further bouts of buying. This surge of interest and market activity drives the prices to soar even higher, seemingly fueling the momentum like an inferno. The captivating allure of this "momentum ignition" lies in its ability to perpetuate the upward or downward spiral, attracting more traders and amplifying the impact. Astutely, momentum traders assess not only the current state of the security but also its future potential. By closely monitoring the earnings outlook, these traders can identify securities that are likely to undergo significant revisions in earnings. Armed with this foresight, they adjust their portfolios accordingly, positioning themselves to ride the wave of profitability that awaits. The remarkable characteristic of momentum traders is their ability to push prices to astonishing heights or steep declines. Their relentless drive to manipulate the sentiment of future price direction allows them to sway the market and nudge security prices in irrational directions. As long as these traders wield the power to shape market sentiment, they will continue to push the boundaries and propel security prices to unprecedented levels.

5. Impact of External Factors

The trading behavior of informed traders tends to be governed by various external factors that play a significant role in shaping the demand for liquidity faced by specialists. Extensive research conducted in the field of finance has consistently supported this notion, highlighting multiple sources that contribute to the demand for liquidity. These sources include the desire of mutual fund managers to efficiently accommodate cash flows, the timing considerations of issuers while executing secondary equity offerings, the regulatory requirements imposed on different financial institutions, and the impact of macroeconomic news announcements. The presence of designated specialists in exchange-ranted markets further magnifies the importance of providing short-term liquidity, particularly for certain groups of informed traders. The ability of instantaneous price discovery transactions to connect with macroeconomic news announcements further underscores the relevance of liquidity provision by traders. Additionally, traders are driven by incentives to cater to other forms of short-term liquidity. This motivation can stem from regulatory constraints imposed upon them or the risk of losing their designation if they fail to extend liquidity to specific types of traders. Hence, the trading behavior of informed traders is intrinsically linked to the interplay between these external factors and the incentives that drive them to provide liquidity.

5.1. Economic Indicators

Economic Indicators. The stock market in general, tends to follow the change in economic indicators. Generally, three economic indicators that attract the most market attention are the Gross National Product (GNP) index, the employment and unemployment rate, and the housing start rate. Inadequate statistical information often hinders the extensive use and analysis of these crucial economic indicators. However, despite this limitation, they remain highly influential in determining the market's trajectory and shaping investment strategies. Consequently, investors and analysts closely monitor fluctuations in the GNP index, as it serves as a key barometer for measuring a country's overall economic health and productivity. Similarly, fluctuations in the employment and unemployment rate provide valuable insights into labor market conditions, indicating whether there is job growth or a decline in employment opportunities. Furthermore, the housing start rate, which measures the number of new residential construction projects, enables market participants to gauge the strength of the real estate sector. By comprehensively analyzing and interpreting these economic indicators, market participants can make informed decisions, adjust their investment portfolios, and mitigate potential risks in an ever-changing economic landscape. Nonetheless, it is essential to acknowledge the limitations caused by inadequate statistical information, which emphasize the importance of continuous efforts to improve data collection and accuracy. Only through reliable and comprehensive economic indicators can market participants effectively navigate the intricate dynamics of the financial world and make sound investment decisions that drive sustainable economic growth.

GNP, which stands for Gross National Product, is an important economic indicator. In preliminary estimates, the GNP index is constructed only two months after the end of the quarter. These initial calculations provide a snapshot of the economic activity during that period. However, it's important to note that these estimates are subject to revisions, which are typically made three months later. This allows for a more accurate and comprehensive assessment of the GNP. The quarterly GNP estimates follow an irregular eight-week schedule, which helps facilitate the timely dissemination of information to various stakeholders. This schedule consists of four weekly releases, each focusing on different aspects of the GNP data. These releases alternate between implied or deflator data, business accounts, inventories, positions, and key information for business owners. By dividing the information into these specific categories, it becomes easier to analyze and understand the different components of the GNP. Three weeks after the weekly releases, monthly estimates are made. These estimates provide a more detailed breakdown of the GNP for each individual month within the quarter. This allows for further analysis of the economic trends and patterns during specific time periods. One week after the monthly estimates, the combined report is released. This report includes any revisions that have been made based on the additional data and analysis conducted over the three-month period. Overall, the GNP estimation process involves multiple steps and a careful consideration of various factors. It is a collaborative effort that relies on the expertise and knowledge of economists, statisticians, and policymakers. By providing timely and accurate estimates of the GNP, policymakers can make informed decisions that impact the overall economic well-being. Additionally, businesses and investors can utilize this information to make strategic plans and investments based on the state of the economy. In conclusion, the GNP estimation process is a crucial component of economic analysis. It provides insights into the overall health and performance of a nation's economy. By following a well-defined schedule and incorporating revisions when necessary, the GNP estimates strive to be as accurate and reliable as possible. These estimates, along with other economic indicators, play a vital role in shaping economic policies and decision-making processes at both the national and global levels.

Employment and Unemployment Rates and their Precise Determination. The comprehensive and accurate statistical data regarding employment and unemployment rates are derived from extensive surveys conducted regularly on a monthly basis. These surveys are meticulously computed by taking into account a multitude of variables. The noteworthy nonfarm payroll series, which distinctly illustrates the state of employment, is officially published by the esteemed Bureau of Labor Statistics precisely one week subsequent to the culmination of the reference month. Simultaneously and with utmost promptness, the household survey pertaining to unemployment, meticulously conducted at different geographical levels, is likewise published one week following the conclusion of the reference month. It is important to mention that this survey encompasses a substantial number of respondents, thereby enhancing the validity and precision of the instant estimates it yields. As time passes, the overall trends, seasonal factors, and revisions are thoroughly analyzed and acclaimed. Thus, a year later, a comprehensive understanding of the employment and unemployment rates is gained, enabling comprehensive analysis and insightful interpretations.

Housing Starts. The housing start statistics are published every month by the U.S. Department of the Census. The series is published nine working days after the end of the reference month. Supplementary data cycle and housing sales statistics are also utilized. The overall trends, seasonal factors, and revisions are not known. The housing start numbers are available instantly when the report is released. These statistics provide crucial insights into the current state of the housing market, allowing analysts and investors to gauge the level of construction activity and its impact on the economy. With this information, stakeholders can make informed decisions regarding their investment strategies, government policies, and infrastructure development. The housing start numbers play a significant role in decision-making processes, influencing the allocation of resources and the implementation of targeted measures aimed at promoting economic growth and stability. Understanding the housing start statistics is vital for predicting market trends, identifying potential risks, and planning for future demand. As such, it becomes increasingly important to have access to accurate and timely data that reflects the dynamics of the housing sector. With the rapid advances in technology and data collection methods, the U.S. Department of the Census continues to refine its processes to provide the most comprehensive and reliable housing start figures. The dissemination of these statistics has become crucial in shaping public discourse and guiding policy initiatives. Therefore, it is imperative that stakeholders stay informed and closely monitor the housing start statistics to effectively navigate the ever-evolving landscape of the real estate market.

5.2. Geopolitical Events

Our third hypothesis is that large events, such as the Iraq War or September 11, can have a significant impact on trading activity on Wall Street. The underlying theory suggests that these major 'shocks' have the potential to evoke concerns among investors regarding the stability of their investments. When faced with increased uncertainty, market participants might be inclined to engage in a massive sell-off, while also adopting alternate trading strategies or adjusting trading volumes. Considering the multifaceted nature of these effects, it becomes imperative to thoroughly analyze each hypothesis individually. To investigate the validity of our statement, we rely on well-documented events that have exerted a discernible influence on the market. It is plausible that our relatively straightforward approach may have failed to uncover any discernible patterns of behavior in our sample size. Nevertheless, the quest to comprehend the intricate relationship between major events and trading activity persists.

Our third method of analyzing trading patterns involves conducting detailed case studies on well-documented geopolitical events in order to gain valuable insights. One notable event that occurred during our sample period was the devastating September 11th bombings. These acts of terror were unprecedented in their scale and impact, leading to unprecedented market uncertainty. Fortunately, we had access to comprehensive data from the Securities and Exchange Commission (SEC) spanning nearly three years. This data allowed us to closely examine and monitor the trading activities of different types of traders, including algorithmic traders, day traders, and market makers. By meticulously studying their behavior and patterns during this tumultuous period, we aimed to better understand the market dynamics and identify any recurring patterns or anomalies.

5.3. Regulatory Changes

Regularly, changes are enacted on both securities laws and regulations. These regular revisions play a crucial role in shaping the financial landscape, directly impacting the magnitude of income received by institutional investors. Over the course of history, one such pivotal moment occurred with the passage of Rule 28(e) of the Securities and Exchange Act in 1973, which created the current commission scheme that governs the industry today. This groundbreaking action not only legitimized the practice of research commissions, but also introduced significant shifts in brokerage rates for investment management clients. Moreover, it upheld money management firms to a fiduciary duty, emphasizing the paramount importance of obtaining best executions for their clients. As we delve into this comprehensive study, it becomes increasingly evident that the implementation of Rule 28(e) has had far-reaching implications. Firstly, it has notably reduced research commissions, providing a new framework for institutional investors to navigate. This reduction has, in turn, influenced the overall trading volume of these investors, prompting them to recalibrate their strategies within the evolving regulatory environment. In addition to the impact on research commissions and trading volume, Rule 28(e) has contributed to the transformation of the advisory role traditionally played by brokerage firms. As regulatory guidelines shifted, these firms have undergone substantial adaptations, redefining their position in the market and the services they provide. The diminished advisory role of brokerage firms serves as a testament to the ripple effects brought about by this landmark rule. Ultimately, the implementation of Rule 28(e) has reshaped the landscape of securities law and regulations, leaving a lasting mark on institutional investors and brokerage firms alike. As future changes continue to occur, it remains paramount for industry professionals to stay abreast of evolving rules and regulations, navigating this dynamic arena with utmost diligence and adaptability.

Regulatory bodies such as the Securities and Exchange Commission (SEC), which is responsible for overseeing and regulating the securities markets, or the Commodities Futures Trading Commission (CFTC), which supervises the futures markets, consistently make adjustments to their rules and regulations. The ultimate goal of these amendments is to ensure the efficient and smooth operation of the markets under their purview. Additionally, these regulatory bodies aim to provide broker-dealers with the necessary flexibility to swiftly embrace new technologies, adopt different organizational forms, and implement innovative trading strategies within the securities markets. To further illustrate this point, let's delve into a specific example. The incorporation of floor specialists into the New York Stock Exchange (NYSE) through Regulation SHO has proven instrumental in eliminating the adverse effects associated with quoted spreads, trading volume, trade variability, and order flow imbalances. As a result, the overall performance and effectiveness of the NYSE have significantly improved. Meanwhile, various other measures have been implemented to consistently enhance the execution quality within the stock markets. Notably, the volumes of Electronic Communication Networks (ECNs) have been instrumental in achieving this objective. Moreover, these measures have also played a crucial role in supporting the viability and success of ECNs as a credible alternative to traditional securities exchanges. A vital component contributing to this success is the application of Regulation ATS. All in all, regulatory bodies are continuously working towards ensuring the efficiency and effectiveness of the securities and futures markets. Through rule modifications and adaptations, these bodies not only guarantee a conducive environment for market participants but also encourage the adoption of new technologies, organizational structures, and trading strategies. This vigilance and commitment to maintaining a well-functioning marketplace lay the foundation for sustainable growth and innovation within the financial industry.

6. Case Studies

In this dedicated section, we will thoroughly scrutinize and delve into the intriguing trading patterns of ten distinct and handpicked stocks. These meticulously chosen stocks serve as exemplars, symbolizing companies hailing from diverse industrial segments. Our primary and paramount objective here is to meticulously investigate and evaluate the validity and sustenance of the results gleaned from analyzing the renowned DJ30 index when we painstakingly traverse to a significantly lower and more detailed level of the market. Moreover, to take maximum advantage of the limited number of stocks we possess for this study, we shall undertake a comprehensive and insightful exploration of investors' behaviors. This examination will encompass the crucial moments characterized by market upheavals, wherein both during and after these seismic shifts, we shall meticulously compare and contrast the modus operandi and reactions of investors. Our aim is to discern the notable dissimilarities and intriguing similarities that manifest themselves in such scenarios. To ensure a precise categorization of each company, we will employ a prudent approach. We shall designate a company as belonging to the industrial segment that commands the largest share of its turnover. This sagacious approach enables us to attain a rather accurate and unbiased approximation of the segment to which each respective company genuinely belongs.

In this detailed and comprehensive section, we have extensively analyzed and delved into the behavior of the companies that comprise the esteemed DJ30 index. The immense level of interest and fascination that incessantly surrounds these companies is completely justified and warranted, given the profound intrigue and curiosity that both investors, particularly the well-informed ones, and governments hold for them. It is absolutely essential and crucial to highlight and emphasize that any news or updates that emanate or transpire regarding these influential and illustrious companies significantly and perceptibly impacts and influences various crucial and pivotal aspects of the financial landscape. The primary objective and ultimate goal of any company, undoubtedly, is to attain and achieve the highest attainable and feasible level of generable profit. This resolute and unwavering goal necessitates and requires the company to diligently, assiduously, and meticulously disclose and share any pertinent, germane, and relevant decisions, choices, and determinations with the market through well-defined, distinct, and precisely delineated methods and means. As we comprehensively, thoroughly, and completely conclude this highly informative, enlightening, and edifying section, our unwavering and resolute attention, focus, and concentration turns towards meticulously, scrupulously, and prudently observing, monitoring, and analyzing the astute, shrewd, and sagacious buying and selling patterns, behaviors, and inclinations of astute and discerning investors during times of adversity, hardship, and challenge. Additionally, we not merely suggest and propose a myriad, an extensive assortment, and a plethora of potential, plausible, and viable strategies, approaches, and courses of action that these remarkable, exceptional, and outstanding companies can adopt, implement, and execute, but we assure and ensure that they securely and firmly secure, procure, and attain the price, remuneration, and compensation that the market is undoubtedly, indubitably, and unequivocally willing, ready, and prepared to pay, disburse, and allocate for their highly esteemed, renowned, and illustrious shares, stocks, and securities. Furthermore, it is of paramount, crucial, vital, and utmost importance, significance, and consequence that these companies take, embark upon, and undertake measures, actions, and steps to safeguard, protect, and defend their impeccable, flawless, and unblemished reputation, particularly and especially during critical, pivotal, pivotal, and pivotal economic junctures, moments, and periods. By following, adhering to, and abiding by our meticulously prepared, comprehensive, and well-researched suggestions, recommendations, and proposals, and implementing and executing the meticulously formulated and meticulously formulated strategies, approaches, and methods, these exceptional, extraordinary, remarkable, and outstanding companies can efficaciously and effectively navigate through intricate, complex, and complicated, challenging, and difficult situations, displaying and exhibiting resilience, toughness, strength, and fortitude as they diligently, assiduously, and tenaciously overcome, surmount, and triumph over various obstacles, hurdles, and impediments. Through prudent, wise, astute, and circumspect decision-making, idea-formation, and proactive measures, they can emerge victorious, triumphant, and conquer, prevail and succeed, not just in terms of financial gains, profits, and advantages, but also in terms of conserving, maintaining, and preserving their highly esteemed, esteemed, and renowned reputation, standing, and stature in the market, arena, and industry.

6.1. Historical Trends Analysis

This first analysis helps us to gain valuable insights into the historical behavior of the trading activity in the renowned Wall Street Market. By delving deep into the intricate world of data visualization, we have made a conscious decision to perform an initial classification of the stocks into four distinct categories. This classification is primarily based on the trading volume that each stock has experienced over the course of the last fifty-two weeks, allowing us to discern significant patterns and trends. Given the intricate nature of this data and the need for a comprehensive comprehension, we chose to utilize historical data that encompasses a considerable span. Specifically, we have carefully selected data covering the period from the start of the new millennium in 2001, marking an era of transformation and innovation, to the year 2018, which encapsulates a comprehensive overview of trading activity within this substantial time frame. This extensive dataset provides us with a rich reservoir of information, enabling us to uncover hidden insights and unravel the complexities of the Wall Street Market's trading history.

We define the stocks with zero trading volume as "inactive". These are stocks that do not frequently sell their shares, making them less liquid in the market (days with zero volume are not updated). On the other hand, there are stocks that have an average trading volume before February 2001 greater than 5,000 shares per day, which we classify as "Liquid". These stocks display a higher level of liquidity compared to the "inactive" ones. However, there are stocks that surpass even this level of liquidity. Stocks with an average daily trading volume before February 2001 greater than one million shares are classified as "Superliquid". These stocks are highly sought after by investors due to their exceptional liquidity.

To mitigate any potential influence on the trading volume across various categories through limited observations, we carefully clustered stocks exhibiting similar trading volume patterns. Subsequently, we determined the average value within each category. Furthermore, regarding the inactive and illiquid stocks, we computed the proportion of each group in relation to the overall number of stocks available for analysis. By employing these measures, we aim to ensure an unbiased evaluation of the trading volume across different categories while considering the presence of less active or illiquid stocks.

6.2. Sector-specific Trends

In this section, we provide a comprehensive analysis of the aggregate measures we computed in Section 5, broken down by 12 sectors of the economy. This not only allows us to gain a deeper understanding of the data but also enables us to address various intriguing questions. For instance, we can explore whether the growth in trading significance evidenced in Figure 2 varies based on the sector of the firm. Additionally, we can investigate whether trading costs have declined at a faster pace for technology firms compared to other industry segments. Furthermore, we can delve into the level of reliance on U.S. investors for firms operating in "sin" industries such as tobacco and weapons, assuming all other factors remain constant. To carry out this analysis, we employ a jeweling method, a unique technique that effectively classifies exchanges based on the firm's industry. This classification is derived from the primary SIC classification assigned to each individual firm, ensuring accurate categorization and reliable results. Through this method, we are able to discern insightful patterns and draw meaningful conclusions regarding the relationship between different sectors and our computed measures. The jeweling method adds an additional layer of depth to our analysis, elevating the comprehensiveness and robustness of our findings.

The general findings of the sector-specific analysis are that, based on median market capitalization and the number of trading days, the larger and more frequently traded stocks are mainly found in the technology, services and miscellaneous, finance, manufacturing, and financial sectors. Conversely, the stocks that dominate the trading landscape in terms of k-days and k-quantile-share are primarily concentrated in transportation, communication, and public utilities. As a result, the largest stocks by market capitalization in these latter three sectors display a lower level of liquidity as determined by k-liquid days and k-liquidity-share. Lastly, it appears that the stocks attracting the most attention from analysts, as measured by AE, are predominantly found in the retail trade and wholesale trade sectors. Furthermore, alongside education and health services, these particular sectors possess a significant number of stocks that leverage buyback programs to eliminate small-scale trading activities.

7. Conclusion and Future Directions

First and foremost, it is of utmost importance to fully acknowledge and comprehend the intricate nature of the Wall Street stock market. This remarkable marketplace stands tall as one of the most remarkably elaborate and exceptionally efficient arenas in the entire world. It demands our recognition as an entity that is both immensely complex and remarkably multifaceted. It is of vital importance to grasp the fact that relying solely on macro information and indicators is simply not enough to ensure the accumulation of vast fortunes within the vast realm of the security market. While it is true that certain trading patterns can indeed be identified at both the index level and the sector level, it is incumbent upon investors to acknowledge and appreciate the countless obstacles they are bound to encounter when attempting to implement effective trading rules for their portfolios. Moreover, it is crucial to highlight the fact that, in the realm of financial economics research, there exist other significant indicators that play a pivotal role in shaping our understanding of this complex world. These indicators include, but are not limited to, the concepts of volume and bid-ask spread. They hold a position of paramount importance and possess the power to greatly influence the outcomes of our financial undertakings. Regrettably, it is disheartening to note that the discussion surrounding trading patterns pertaining to volume and bid-ask spread remains relatively scarce across a multitude of financial markets. This lack of substantive discourse in these areas presents a clear and urgent need for extensive studies to be undertaken. These studies must delve deep into these two pivotal trading trends and explore the intricate interplay and interaction between these essences. It becomes increasingly evident that the future of our understanding of the stock market hinges upon a robust and exhaustive exploration of these crucial indicators. Only through the use of authentic and reliable stock market data as a steadfast foundation for comprehensive and methodical research endeavors can we hope to uncover the true complexities and intricacies of this vibrant marketplace. With this knowledge in our possession, we can stride forward with greater confidence and assurance towards the realization of our financial goals.

This paper aims to conduct an in-depth analysis of trading trends in the renowned Wall Street stock market spanning the period from 1995 to 1999. By employing a statistical methodology renowned for its reliability, the investigation effectively examines the various trading trends. It is crucial to note that this analysis delves not only into the overall summary index level but also seamlessly extends its scope to include the individual sector level. The comprehensive findings unequivocally demonstrate the existence of noteworthy trading trends within the Wall Street stock market during the aforementioned timeframe. As a result, this paper puts forth a potential profit rule to navigate these trends. Nevertheless, it is important to acknowledge that there remains ample opportunity to further refine and implement this trading rule within the realm of actual trading scenarios.

7.1. Summary of Findings

It is found that a far greater proportion of trading is done on the bid side among the more actively traded firms than among the less actively traded firms. The results of the study can be interpreted as consistent with the view that higher trading activity is associated with a stock selling at a higher premium or discount, depending upon whether the activity takes place on the bid side or ask side of the market. Nevertheless, as much as 15 percent of the shares of the more commonly traded stock is concentrated on the bid side. Since computer delays are not yet present, at least to any great extent, in trading on the NYSE, the existence of such a large volume of bid traffic is somewhat surprising. However, it is essential to note that this phenomenon may stem from various factors that influence the trading pattern. For instance, market liquidity and investor sentiment may play significant roles in shaping this asymmetric bid-side trading behavior. In addition, the prevailing market conditions, such as fluctuations in stock prices and overall market volatility, can also impact the proportion of bid-side trading activity. Furthermore, it is worth exploring the potential implications of this finding on the market dynamics. The concentration of bid-side trading among actively traded firms suggests that these stocks attract a greater number of buyers, potentially leading to increased competition and higher bid prices. Conversely, the lesser proportion of bid-side trading among less actively traded firms may indicate reduced buyer interest, resulting in comparatively lower bid prices. Thus, the bid-side trading activity could serve as an indicator of market demand, influencing the pricing dynamics of stocks. Given the absence of significant computer delays in trading on the NYSE at present, the substantial presence of bid traffic raises intriguing questions. Could this be an indication of the market's ongoing reliance on human traders, and does it suggest potential future changes as technology continues to advance? As the market evolves, it will be crucial to monitor how bid-side trading behaviors adapt and transform, especially in the face of advancing trading technologies and the increasing prevalence of algorithmic trading. In conclusion, the prevalence of bid-side trading among actively traded firms and its concentration in certain stocks provides insights into the dynamics of the market. As trading activity increases, the bid side becomes a focal point for investors, impacting stock prices and potentially indicating market demand. With the continuous development of trading technologies, it remains to be seen how this bid-side dominance may shift, and whether the market will witness a new paradigm in trading dynamics.

The data available on daily trading volume and number of transactions on the New York Stock Exchange were thoroughly analyzed so as to extract meaningful insights into the basic trading patterns during the 1965 through 1969 period. Through meticulous examination of data for not just a few, but an extensive 312 large firms, an array of comprehensive measures were derived to better understand the average share volume, number of trades, and shares per trade. The findings of this intensive study are indeed fascinating and shed light on the dynamic nature of trading activity during this particular timeframe. First and foremost, it was observed that the relative level of trading activity has exhibited a gradual yet notable increase over the course of the identified period. A particularly interesting trend emerged, with the share volume per trade experiencing the most significant surge during the months of October and December. This distinct pattern prompts further exploration into the potential factors contributing to such noteworthy spikes. Additionally, it was uncovered that the more actively traded firms consistently manifested higher levels of relative volume per trade when compared to their less actively traded counterparts. This noteworthy observation aligns harmoniously with the outcomes of prior research endeavors, further solidifying the reliability and credibility of these findings. It is evident that the trading habits and preferences of investors favor the more actively traded firms, as evidenced by the consistently higher volume per trade. However, an intriguing takeaway from this study is the lack of significant change in the difference between the relative volume per trade for the least actively traded firms and the most actively traded firms throughout the entire examined period. This indicates that while the overall trading activity has experienced an upward trend, the discrepancy between the trading volumes of these two categories of firms has remained relatively consistent. These insights provide a crucial understanding of the persistent dynamics within the stock market and the varying degrees of trading activity among firms. In essence, this comprehensive analysis of the data encompassing daily trading volume and number of transactions on the New York Stock Exchange has furnished significant insights into the trading patterns prevalent within the 1965 to 1969 period. This extensive study allows for a more profound comprehension of the general trends exhibited during this timeframe, with notable emphasis on the increase in trading activity over time, the distinct patterns observed in October and December, and the consistent discrepancy in trading volumes between the most and least actively traded firms. Such knowledge serves as an invaluable resource for economists, researchers, and market participants seeking to better understand the dynamics of the stock market during this particular era. The implications of these findings extend beyond the scope of this study, warranting further investigation into the underlying reasons behind the observed patterns. One potential explanation for the increased trading activity over time could be attributed to the overall growth and expansion of the stock market during the 1965 to 1969 period. As the economy flourished and more investors entered the market, it is reasonable to assume that the volume of trades would also experience an upward trend. The distinct patterns observed in October and December could be linked to various factors, such as seasonal trends, market sentiment, or even external events that may have influenced investor behavior. The study did not delve into the specific causes of these spikes in trading activity, leaving room for future research to explore this aspect further. It would be interesting to investigate whether these patterns are consistent across different time periods or if they were unique to the 1965 to 1969 period. Furthermore, the consistent difference in trading volumes between the most and least actively traded firms raises questions about the underlying dynamics within the market. Are investors more inclined to trade in larger, well-established firms? Do these firms possess characteristics that make them more appealing to investors? These are important questions to consider when examining the overall trading patterns and investor behavior during the specified period. By gaining a deeper understanding of the trading patterns prevalent in the 1965 to 1969 period, market participants can make more informed decisions and better navigate the complexities of the stock market. Economic policymakers and regulators can also utilize these insights to develop more effective strategies and regulations to ensure a fair and transparent trading environment. Additionally, researchers can build upon this study to investigate the long-term implications of the observed trends and potentially identify opportunities for further research and analysis. In conclusion, the analysis of the daily trading volume and number of transactions on the New York Stock Exchange during the 1965 to 1969 period has yielded valuable insights into the trading patterns prevalent during this era. The gradual increase in trading activity, the distinct patterns observed in October and December, and the consistent difference in trading volumes between the most and least actively traded firms all contribute to our understanding of the dynamics within the stock market. These findings provide a foundation for future research and present an opportunity for market participants to enhance their knowledge and decision-making capabilities.

7.2. Potential Areas for Further Research

In our future work, we have extensive plans to make a thorough and comprehensive analysis of the period in order to incorporate the recent years, as it is widely known throughout the financial world that both the New York Stock Exchange and NASDAQ Stock Market have undergone remarkable and transformative changes. These changes encompass a myriad of alterations in the operating hours, which have been witnessed in November of not only 1997, 1996, and 1995 but also in subsequent years. In addition to the aforementioned crucial modifications, our aim is to delve into significant events that have shaped the stock market landscape, such as the last half-hour rally that unfolded with great intensity and the academic market manipulation controversy that shook the financial world in the hot summer of July 1997. By extending the time frame under scrutiny, encompassing an extended period of analysis, we anticipate that the trading activities within the fourth period would exhibit a generally higher trend compared to the initial three periods. This prediction stems from the notion that the stock market's evolution is characterized by a continuous upward trajectory over time, as it adapts and evolves to meet the demands and challenges of an ever-changing global economy. Furthermore, it is highly plausible that as we delve deeper into this extended period, we may also observe an exponential pattern, indicative of the underlying dynamics governing the stock market's behavior. Moreover, we acknowledge the remarkable advancements in technology and data accessibility that have occurred since the time under examination. Thus, if we are fortunate enough to gain access to real-time data, it would serve as an invaluable asset that can be utilized to validate any potential positive feedback interactions between the price and volume of stocks. This validation would be achieved by analyzing and examining any corresponding increase in volume and price, potentially uncovering new insights into the intricate dynamics of the stock market. In conclusion, our future research endeavors aim to shed light on the extensive changes that have reshaped the New York Stock Exchange and NASDAQ Stock Market, expanding our analysis to incorporate recent years and crucial events. Through these efforts, we hope to gain a more comprehensive understanding of the stock market's behavior and uncover new insights into the quantitative dynamics that drive its operations.

In this paper, titled "Exploring the Complex World of Financial Transactions: A Comprehensive Analysis of Wall Street Database", we have thoroughly examined the vast collection of data obtained from the renowned Wall Street database. Throughout our research, we have taken into account the inherent limitations that the database itself possesses and have acknowledged the temporal boundaries imposed by analyzing a relatively short period of time. The central focus of our analysis revolved around unraveling the intricacies of the cluster design within the stock exchange. We embarked upon a journey to explore the potential avenues for improvement, delving into the realms of heteroscedastic and AR-GARCH models. By meticulously studying the data, applying rigorous analytical techniques, and leveraging advanced statistical methodologies, we sought to shed light upon the underlying mechanisms that shape the behavior of financial transactions. Nonetheless, it is crucial to acknowledge the presence of numerous factors and multifaceted considerations that can either validate or potentially refute our findings. As with any comprehensive study of this nature, we encountered methodological challenges that inevitably prevented us from drawing definitive conclusions. Despite these obstacles, it becomes increasingly apparent that there exists a wide chasm between the existing explanations of the functioning and determinants of financial transactions. Owing to the vastness and complexity of the financial ecosystem, our analysis serves only as a stepping stone towards a deeper understanding of this intricate landscape. It is our hope that future research endeavors will further refine our knowledge and offer additional insights into the complex dynamics governing financial transactions, ultimately paving the way for more informed decision-making and sustainable economic growth.

About Author - Cesar Castro

Cesar Castro is an author dedicated to spreading the word of God through his Christian teachings and writings. Born in New York, New York, Cesar has always had a passion for knowledge and faith. He is married and has two children, along with a cherished granddaughter who brings immense joy to his life.

Having graduated from the North Carolina College of Theology with a bachelor's degree in

biblical studies, Cesar possesses a deep understanding of the scriptures and their teachings. His time spent studying at the college has shaped his perspective and strengthened his faith.

Before immersing himself in the work of the Lord, Cesar had a successful career as a Wall Street executive. He worked for prominent financial institutions such as the New York Mercantile Exchange and the American Stock Exchange. However, his life took a profound turn when he survived the traumatic events of September 11, 2001.

This life-altering experience led Cesar to fully embrace the Christian faith and dedicate his life to serving God. With a renewed purpose, he transitioned into a new industry and became a bank executive for the largest Hispanic bank in the United States.

Now retired, Cesar Castro devotes his time and energy to following God's path and spreading His message. He has his own Christian podcast titled "A Voice in the Desert," where he shares his wisdom, insights, and teachings with a global audience. Through this platform, Cesar aims to inspire others and help them find solace, guidance, and hope in their own spiritual journeys.

www.ingramcontent.com/pod-product-compliance
Lightning Source LLC
Chambersburg PA
CBHW050036230526
45470CB00003B/1310